THE INVISIBLE

MASK

Dear Leila

Star with your WHY
.... I need to or
i want to ...
and do what you
love
Beata
xty

Beata Bikowska

Disclaimer

Author: Beata Bikowska
Title: The Invisible Mask
ISBN: 978-1-999722326
Category: SELF-HELP/Personal Development/General

Publisher: Breakfree Forever Publishing

Table of Contents

Dedication

I would like to dedicate this book to my children; Alan, Magda, and my beautiful granddaughter Maya, the most beautiful gifts of life.

This dedication would not be completed without dedicating to my mother who, despite many difficulties in her life, always tried to create the best condition for my development. Besides, she gave me the most beautiful gift... my life.

Foreword

People ask me all the time to endorse their books, and I normally say no because I don't know them well enough and feel an endorsement of the book would not be honest. When Beata Bikowska asked me, I didn't hesitate. I said yes!

Why? Because her work on how we wear a mask is ground-breaking. Her work on being real is profound, and the reason she can speak and write with authority on this subject is because she has been there. She has overcome some of life's greatest challenges, she has worn a mask and realised its negative impact, she has been brave and courageous...

Beata has triumphed where many would give up.

I urge you to read her book because it has the capacity to bring awareness and acceptance into your life. It has the capacity to give you realisations that you would be mad not to take notice of, and, if you follow Beata's philosophy and take the mask off, everything can be different.

Nicki Vee

Master Coach Trainer

www.mastercoach.co

Introduction

You will probably agree with me that we have different roles in our lives. We are wearing different masks, depending on the role. We are wearing caps, helmets, and we are covering our bodies in uniforms to become the best example of the role. We become partners, parents, employers, employees, business owners, law officers, and lifesavers. We are holding huge responsibilities depending on the role, as well as the weight of what is hidden behind our mask. Unresolved conflicts, crises, unfulfilled dreams, but more importantly our emotions. Emotions that have a significant impact on our functioning in everyday life, whether personal or professional.

The current image of strong and successful individuals created by the media leaves no space for talk about the price that many people pay for being picture-perfect. The image of being vigilant, being the best and able to achieve everything without any loss is the cause of so much stress. Also, the image of the flawless home, splendid relationship, perfectly-fitting career hides dissatisfaction, fear of rejection and evaluation, as well as emotional difficulties. As you may know, emotional difficulties are responsible for many health problems, life crises, addictions, and even loss of lives. Even so, some people are desperate to fit into this unreal world and to perform their role.

It does not matter how well you would perform your role. The hidden truth can show up in the least expected moment and can cost you a lot. So, do you really need to fit in others' definition of a successful life? Do you really need to look and act like them, even when what you see is only a small part of their life? More importantly, a part created for external necessities only.

Nowadays, we encourage children to express their feelings and needs. We appreciate the honesty of other people, we admire others, but most of us are still afraid of showing our true emotions. Why are we ashamed and afraid of being ourselves? Who are we really frightened of, others or ourselves?

I had the privilege to meet and spent a few days with many successful people. We all came to learn new skills and become masters in our fields. Sharing our stories was part of the programme. And what I noticed? Behind every "mask of success," a real man was hiding. Entrepreneurs, doctors, therapists, accountants, managers, all very successful people, but it does not mean very happy people. People with a smile on their faces and sadness in their hearts. They had great difficulties to talk about real emotions. Why? Because it is not easy to be real in the "artificial world." We often hide behind the titles, the names of positions, the size of the car, but we suffer like everyone else. However, we are worried that we will lose authority by showing humanity. But professionals are humans too.

So, if you read this book thoughtfully, you will find lots of reasons why people hide their "true faces" and how dangerous it is.

Why must you read this book? Because it is based on real experiences. Because you will find not only reasons for hiding true emotions, you will also find different ways to bundle it off.

Why do you have to read it now? Because your life, health, and happiness are more important than the picture of the untruthful world. Because life is short and you do not want to waste any second of it.

Because… "In a world where everyone is wearing masks, it is a privilege to see souls" - Amanda Richardson

CHAPTER ONE

Who is behind the mask

*"We can never obtain peace in the outer world until
we make peace with ourselves."*
Dalai Lama XIV

My name is Beata Bikowska. I am a Health and Life Coach and Motivational Speaker.

I have been working with people for over 25 years, and I am extremely passionate about assisting individuals to set and achieve both their personal and professional goals within all areas of their life from learning, employment, relationships, and their own personal wellbeing. I gained extensive experience across the Health and Social Care sector, working within a wide range of roles from a Staff Nurse, Social Worker, and most recently Health and Life Coach. I have had the honour of accompanying people in various moments of their lives: from sadness to joy, from resignation, falling, fight, and finally victory, to whom many of us, including myself, can relate to and this is what drives my vision and purpose of my work.

I not only have the knowledge and professional experience, but also life experience that many can relate to as I suffered much due to lack of belief in myself that had a significant influence on how I can live and feel. I was able to overcome this lack of confidence and limiting beliefs to achieving my goals and becoming a successful entrepreneur, and these are the many tips and strategies that I now share with the world.

Of course, it has been a long time before I realised that I can live my life as I want to. For many years, I thought that life is how it is and you cannot change it. The life I used to know was not nice and easy. I was born in Poland in the early '70s. I do remember empty shops, limited amount of food, lack of freedom of speech and ubiquitous control. It was a time when alcohol became an exchange product and was regularly overused by many people. Also, it was a time when emotional, verbal, and physical abuse was tolerable. That time, people could not cope with life difficulties in any other ways than that. There was no education on managing emotions and dealing with life challenges. Any consultation with a psychologist or psychiatrist was stigmatised, but… violence was allowed.

Growing up in an unhealthy and unsafe environment had a detrimental impact on how I saw myself and the world around me.

If you would have been with me in the 1970s, you would have seen the late, dark night. Old tenement house. A few years old girl lying in bed. Despite the fact that our flat is on the second floor, I am aware of every single sound on the street; cats purring, tree noise. I can hear his steps on the stairway. He is coming back. I can hear my heart beats. Is he going to his room? No. He shouts, using words that a child should never hear. Broken glass in the kitchen, door slam. Mum, where is mum? ...in her room, pretending to be asleep. Even so, he talks to her. He wants money; he wants more vodka. She is up and getting out of his way. I am still in bed with my head under the pillow. I am shaking. I am scared. I cannot cope with it again. Night by night, week by week, for years. Another broken glass, another curse. Will he come to my room? Will he hurt me? I don't know. He never did, but who knows. I saw blood on his hands. I saw him kicking walls. I am scared. I cannot deal with this fear anymore. I have to go, but where? ...I am sitting on the stairs that lead to the attic. It is cold. No shoes, no socks... Silence, finally silence. I can return to my bed. Couple hours of sleep and school. Maths test today.

I am back home. A warm dinner on the table, clean house. It looks like nothing happened. No one talks about it. Was it real? When I tried to open my mouth, I was told not to create any drama. So, no words, no emotions. Perfectly looking house, flawlessly arranged hair and ironed clothes, a smile on the face and silence. Another silence before the storm. It was difficult to understand those mixed messages and all accompanying emotions. More, it was so difficult to hide those emotions; anxiety, fear, tension, confusion, sadness, shame... So, wearing a mask was the only way to handle it.

Have you ever felt unable to show your real emotions?

I was a middle-grade student until I started medical school and practised as a nurse. I graduated from this school with honours, so it was a sign that I am able to achieve something and

I can have a positive future despite all those guesses... did people make comments or try to predict your future; unsuccessful future because of your upbringing?

I fell in love with nursing. Looking after people, helping them, saving their lives and assisting in very difficult moments became a part of me; I discovered my passion. You would not believe, but it was a time when I was not aware of hoist existence. My muscles, my spine became a machine many times a day until I refused to work. That day, I ended up in a hospital bed with a severe back injury. My world was falling apart. I felt that I would not be able to assist people anymore. I felt that something important for me is going to end. However, the end became the start of a new journey. I was transferred to work on the addiction ward. It was a time when I had a better understanding of this world, but being around drunk people still caused me tremendous anxiety. But as you can imagine, I became a master of hiding my emotions. Nevertheless, it was a time when the universe decided that I need to face my fear. As the nursing role was very limited, I had the opportunity to spend more time with people and listen to their stories. My knowledge about addiction was good, but during those conversations, I learned more than I could ever ask for. When I deeply melt the mechanism of addiction and the impact of the environment on our lives, I decided to assist more people. I became a social worker. Having a vast knowledge and more importantly, my personal experiences, I was able to build a good rapport with my clients. I was trusted and felt invited into people's lives; I witnessed sadness and happiness, life and death, ups and downs. My clients always felt well understood and supported.

However, I faced many situations when people tried to push my boundaries, both in personal and professional life. It was not easy to remain calm, but at that time, I thought I had no choice. It was better to keep quiet instead of "creating a drama." So, the only way to manage it was to keep the mask on. I always kept a smile on my face, although my life was falling apart. I always tried to keep all in. When I accidentally opened up, I felt bad. I was concentrating on what I should or should not, instead of what I need and want. This kind of behaviour is typical for those who grow up in a dysfunctional environment. They often think about others instead of about themselves. They want to please everyone in order to keep everyone calm and happy. Also, this a coping mechanism in order to take control and deal with enormous internal distress.

Today, I know that holding this mask on for so long not only poisoned my body, but it also poisoned my life. Yes, I became physically and mentally unwell. I experienced a huge number of unexplained physical difficulties, low mood, lack of energy and motivation. This had a significant impact on my personal and professional life. Being unable to perform on daily tasks scared me very much. Especially the moment when I recognised that I am hiding from loved ones, as to put the fake smile on became impossible. I knew it that I need to do something about it.

As an expert of "other people's lives," I have decided to examine mine. It became obvious that what I am going through is a product of a few perspectives. It became apparent that past trauma, low self-esteem, and long-term stress are responsible for my health and illness. It has been evident that the time of life purification has arrived...

Once I realised that showing my true emotions is not only important, but also necessary to remain physically and mentally well, my personal and professional life has changed. The fact that I am a wife, mother, grandmother, and professional does not take my right to express my true emotions. Every single role requires appropriate appearance, but it does not deprive me of the right to express myself. Yes, it professionally requires to keep my personal opinion separately, but it does not require to forget who I am... I am human.

CHAPTER 2

Acceptance

"Acceptance of one's life has nothing to do with resignation; it does not mean running away from the struggle. On the contrary, it means accepting it as it comes, with all the handicaps of heredity, of suffering, of psychological complexes and injustices."
Paul Tournier

One of the most difficult problems that people hide behind the mask is self-acceptance.

What does self-acceptance mean? It is accepting yourself fully for the person you truly are. It means to accept what you like or dislike about yourself. It means being honest with yourself. It means to accept the way you look, the way you think, act, and react.

The biggest misunderstanding about self-acceptance is that people think they need to like everything about themselves. As mentioned earlier, self-acceptance includes acceptance of what we dislike. It could be something that you are not proud of: for example, your words, your behaviour, your limitation, your mistakes. We all make mistakes, and we are not perfect. But to admit and accept the fact will help you to feel better about yourself.

Also, self- acceptance includes acceptance of your past. Acceptance of what you have experienced, your family, and the way you grew up. It includes acceptance of the place you were born, your parents, your siblings, and the wider family as it did not depend on you. Also, acceptance of what happened to you. It does not mean to ignore the wrong done to you. It means to admit, accept, and forgive it. It does not mean to forget, but to not allow the past to determine your future. Moreover, to not allow your past to determine your health as negative emotions cause a lot of diseases and illnesses. It has been proven that worries, stress, and anxiety trigger adrenaline and cortisone. Whereas those hormones affect your heart, breathing, skin, muscles, and immune system. It has not only been proven by doctors, but I also witnessed it in my professional work, and more importantly, I experienced it myself until I realised that there is no need for it.

Constantly thinking about my past resulted in low self-esteem. I focused on the negatives, and I have been judging myself more than anyone else. Also, I became an expert in writing "dark scenarios"; when there was peace in my life, I was subconsciously waiting for the storm. Also, when I was successful, the success I was achieving was inversely proportional to what I thought about myself. I thought that what I have in my life is not my accomplishment, it is actually a coincidence and certainly, in a moment, the whole world will see how hopeless I am. Why? Because people with low self-esteem are instilled in negative messages during childhood. Sometimes, in the form of clear verbal messages, such as "you would not achieve anything" or "you are nothing, not good enough," but sometimes by treating the child that it felt unimportant, underestimated, or invisible.

Likewise, very demanding parents could employ huge pressure on their child. The child forgets about his needs, dreams, and plans, all to satisfy his parents. If the child is unable to meet these expectations, punishment usually arises. Parents do not hide their disappointment, and the child feels responsible for their bad mood. Those children, and later adults, stop listening to themselves and concentrate on meeting the expectations of others. Lastly, they try to deserve or to buy acceptance of others.

Negative messages have destructive power. They are like information recorded in the mind, which are often activated in the least expected situations, even when an adult already has to appreciate and enjoy his achievements.

So, why self-acceptance is important? It is so important because if you do not accept yourself for who you really are, you will create many problems in your life. Some of these problems are affecting you personally (low self-esteem, unhappiness) and some will affect how others treat you (becoming a victim). Also, some people struggle to accept who they are and then try to be like someone else.

Self-acceptance is the opposite to self-judgment. If you judge yourself constantly, this can lead to anxiety and depression or other mental health difficulties. Also, self-acceptance releases you from the concern of what other people think about you or even more from, what you think other people think about you. So, it is worth taking a look at your own childhood and understanding the mechanism of a distorted, inadequate vision of yourself. Knowledge and understanding of the cause help to find the tools to deal with this problem.

Is there something that you are still having a difficulty accepting?

Self-acceptance is a process and sometimes requires professional assistance. Do not be afraid to ask for help. We are asking for help to remain strong not because we are weak.

However, I would like to share some tips with you to help you start the process today.

Tips for self-acceptance

You have to accept who you really are. It needs to be a very conscious decision as this is a first and most crucial step before you will start your new journey. Take time to think about who you are – your personality, your background; acknowledge it and accept it. To fully accept yourself, you must accept your limitations and know your own needs, aspirations, and dreams, and to give yourself the right to mistakes. Be able to accept the dissimilarity of others and be open to change. Be able to smile at self and distance yourself from your own failures. Rename failure, rename past. Failure is an event; it is not a person. So learn from it and move on. Stop comparing yourself with others. You do not know what is really going on in someone's life. Accept your imperfection. You cannot be good with everything, and it is impossible to know everything. If you think that you know everything, you know nothing. Concentrate on your strengths, and accept the weakness. Discover what makes you unique. Make a list of things that you are good at and what gives you great pleasure. Be grateful. Appreciate more. Be kind to yourselves, treat yourself well, and do things just for yourself. It is not selfish to have Me time. Believe that you are perfect the way you are. Be yourself.

Moreover, remember, you cannot change the past, but you can create the future. Life will become a better place once you allow yourself to live fully.

CHAPTER 3

Fulfilment

"Don't wait for the perfect moment.
Take the moment and make it perfect."
~Unknown

If you cannot accept yourself and if the opinion of others is important to you, you may have a problem with achieving your own goals and feeling fulfilled.

What is Fulfilment? One will say warm and clean house, big garden, husband, children. Another one will say own a company, money, success. Or maybe everything together? After years of working hard, I woke up one day to realise that I was there. I was married, I had my own house and fulltime, well-paid job. I felt that I had everything I thought I wanted. There was only one, but… the artificially created image of happiness and success.

It does not matter if you are working for someone or you run your own business. If you are an ambitious man or woman, you want more, and you go further. You will fight for your goals every day. You are perceived as a perfect man or a strong woman. However, under each of these terms, your real self hides. You, who obviously want to meet trends and environmental pressures. You, who want to grow and succeed. As well, you who need a cuddle, love, and feel safe. You, who want to accompany children in the most important moments of their lives. You, who suffer secretly, fighting how to merge everything, how to be everywhere, to be for everyone and… to be the best.

Have you ever seen scales or other devices that measure "being good, better, or the best?" Who publishes such ratings? You alone, right? Nobody said that what I was doing was too little or enough. It was me who had to do morñe.

So, I was there. I felt that I had more than I could imagine and yet… I was unsatisfied. The strong pressure of being the best, managing everything without any expense or complains and the emphasis to fit in others' definition of success and happiness took away the joy of family life and my real achievements. It left me with sadness and disappointment; also, it impacted on my health. A few years of visiting specialists, many tests… Over two years of taking meds with no effects.

… Study showed that lack of fulfilment presents itself in general pessimism, lack of motivation, lack of sleep or stimulants. Also, in the absence of willingness to work and active social life, withdrawal, and apathy. It can decrease creativity and impact on your commitment. It could manifest in the loss of appetite or compulsive overeating. Also, in emotional reactions, such as irritation and anger, even verbal aggression. More so, it can create marital and family problems. Besides, it can manifest feelings of gradual exhaustion and increasing body fatigue. Those health difficulties are a cry for help from a tired and stressed body and mind. These are physical symptoms, such as dizziness and headaches, burning chest, nausea, loss of sexual performance, as well as heart or digestive system diseases. Frequent infections, as well as anxiety and depression…

So, again, I put the mask on to hide what I was really struggling with… lack of fulfilment. However, I dreamed that it would happen someday.

Then, the day has arrived.

At the time, I did not think it was such a fantastic experience. I felt unwell, unhappy, unmotivated, sad, and felt like a ship that is sinking. The perfect image of a successful and happy life was so far from reality. That day, I realised that it was not my image. It was not my life. That day, I recognised that I was melting in other people's expectations and their definition of happiness. That day, I recognised the reasons for my unhappiness and lack of gratefulness. That day, I felt I had to throw away what drags me down and to start my own journey. That day, I have decided not to hide anymore and to be real. On that day, I decided to create my own definition of a happy life.

I have decided to:
Set up healthy and strong boundaries

Boundaries are invisible walls between one and the outside world. Boundaries are guidelines, rules, or limits that a person creates to identify reasonable and safe ways for other people to behave towards them and how they will respond when someone exceeds those limits. The best way to determine your boundaries is to think about your personal and professional life, as well as the involvement of others in your definition of success.

To move away from what was draining me

If you are engaged in work or a relationship that drains, disappoints, and discourages you, it is wrong for you. It does not matter how much you've invested in it. It will cost you even more by existing in something that does not work for you. Do not be afraid to change it.

To find my support network

To live up to the imagination of picture-perfect image, people are intensely self-focused. They are dedicating huge amounts of time and energy to expanding their skills and rising to the top. However, they are forgetting about the importance of positive relationships with supporting and empowering people. People that will not only support them in crisis, but will also encourage and motivate them to achieve professional and personal goals on an everyday basis.

To stop worrying about everything

Everyone worries. Worrying can even be helpful when it forces you to take action and solve a problem. But if you are preoccupied with "what if" and "worst-case scenarios," worry becomes a problem. It can deprive your emotional energy, increase the level of anxiety and the impact on your daily life. It can leave you feeling restless, cause insomnia, headaches, stomach problems, muscle tension, and make it difficult to concentrate at work or home. You may take your negative feelings out on others, and you may self-medicate with alcohol or drugs. Chronic worrying can lead to anxiety, nervousness, and a general sense of restlessness. But chronic worrying is a mental habit that can be broken. You can learn how to stay calm and look at life from a less fearful perspective.

To do what I am passionate about

We all need food and pay bills. It is understandable that we all need money to meet our needs. But you will experience different pleasure and different feelings about it by making money on your passion.

Moreover, how do you want to feel successful without feeling satisfied? Is there any satisfaction without passion?

To be grateful for what I have

We are all looking for that thing that will give us deep fulfilment. You can make up your mind to focus only on the bad stuff, or you can acknowledge the beauty around you and be grateful for. So, take your time to admit with appreciation what you love about your life. By appreciating the small things, you will discover a beautiful big world.

Health, Passion, Satisfaction; it drives my action. Beata Bikowska

What does fulfilment mean to me today? It means to be a better version of myself every day, but still being me. It means a free expression of my feelings and my needs. It is a clear set of boundaries, doing what I love. It is a happy family. It is also fulfilling my dreams, achieving my goals, including professional ones. But most importantly, it is living in harmony with myself, not with this artificial world and the expectations of others.

CHAPTER 4

Assertiveness

"To be passive is to let others decide for you. To be aggressive is to decide for others. To be assertive is to decide for yourself. And to trust that there is enough, that you are enough."
Edith Eva Eger

It would seem that the problem of the lack of assertiveness is quite common in society. Unfortunately, people often misunderstand this issue. It has been widely accepted that the lack of assertiveness is simply saying "No" in a situation when we disagree with something or we want to refuse. This is not the lack of assertiveness.

Assertiveness means standing up for your personal rights, expressing thoughts, feelings, and beliefs in a direct, honest, open, and proactive way. Also, assertiveness includes being able to admit your mistakes and to apologise. Being assertive means to possess the ability to say "yes" as this is just as important as the ability to say "no." Also, we are assertive when we are able to accept praise, criticism, and when we can ask for help.

Overestimating the importance of assertiveness in everyday life is difficult. This skill at work will help us to better build our careers in social life, build better relationships with others, and finally reduce the amount of stress. It can help you to express yourself without unnecessary anxiety and more importantly to act in your own best interest. Assertiveness requires certainty that what you think and feel is important. Assertiveness is the ability to reject false beliefs about yourself and to adopt a sense of strength and self- confidence.

Being assertive is different from being passive, aggressive, or manipulative.

A passive person allows others to cross their boundaries. He often agrees to do things that he does not feel like or give others credit for his achievements. Also, he has a problem with asking for help. Moreover, he might over analyse his decision, and he will be worried about other people's opinion. He is ashamed to admit his mistakes and feels uncomfortable talking about his difficulties. He chooses to say nothing and suppress negative emotions, until at some point accumulated anger will simply break out. The suppression of negative emotions causes aggression, which in some situation is completely out of control for the individual. An aggressive person does not respect others and expresses his view violently. Moreover, the lack of an assertive attitude often disturbs the functioning of the individual in society. This person, being at the same time an executioner (being angry) and victim (being passive), withdraws and isolates himself from the environment. Being assertive is different from being manipulative too. Manipulation is a form of using "encouragement" on a person or on a group in such a way that it unconsciously and willingly realises our goals. Manipulation is balancing between docility and aggression, depending on the purpose.

Where does the lack of assertiveness come from? Usually due to lack of satisfying important psychological needs, such as the need for acceptance, security, or belonging to a group. People feel isolated and unstable, so consequently, they are unable to express their needs and wishes. They also learn to respond in a non-assertive way, through experience or how they were brought up. Lack of assertiveness comes from the fact that the child has no opportunity to learn how to speak without fear of what he feels and thinks.

As you might remember, I grew up in a society where children's voice was not vital. I learned that what I think or feel was not important. And every attempt ended in rebuke. I remember those accumulated emotions and helplessness, sometimes even anger. I felt like a balloon that could break. However, it took longer than I thought and it cost more than it should.

Being unable to speak up can have long-lasting negative consequences.

Long-term concealment and suppression of emotions destructively affect health, both psychologically and physically. A person who has not developed an assertive attitude, more often than others, falls into depression, anxiety, or neurosis. An extreme lack of assertive attitude, in the long run, leads to numerous ailments and diseases, such as migraine, sleep disorders, digestive disease, and hypertension. At work, the person becomes less creative and remains shameful, shy, and dependent on interpersonal relationships. Also, such individual remains indecisive and submissive, which makes them easy to manipulate. Internally, they are afraid of competition, criticism, and being involved in a conflict.

Also, many factors may contribute to the lack of assertiveness. Certain roles are associated with non-assertive behaviour. For example, the traditional role of women. Research shows that "stereotypically, women are seen as passive, while men are expected to be more aggressive." People who are stressed or anxious can also act passively or aggressively to protect themselves.

Similarly, some people believe that they cannot change the way they respond. But this is an incorrect assumption. Assertiveness can be developed. Everybody can learn to be more assertive despite their tendencies and situation they are in.

How to become more assertive

It is not easy to become assertive, but it is possible. There are two essential components to becoming more assertive: Firstly, you have to learn to treat yourself with respect. Secondly, you need to work on your communication skills, and you need to respect others too.

So, to become more assertive, you need to:

1. Value yourself and your rights.
   To be more assertive, you need to gain a good understanding of yourself. You need to know your values.

2. Communicate your needs and wants confidently.
   You need to give yourself the right to express your needs and

feelings. Do not assume that someone will automatically know what you need. Be specific, clear, and respectful.

3. Learn to express yourself in a positive way.
It is important to say what is on your mind, even when you have a difficult or negative issue to deal with. But you must do it constructively and sensitively.

4. Be open to criticism and compliments.
Accept both positive and negative feedback.

5. Learn to say "No" and "Yes."
Saying "No" is hard to do, but it is vital if you want to become more assertive.

But do not forget; assertiveness is not about saying no. It is also about saying yes, admitting your mistakes and asking for help. It is not easy, but it is possible. More so, it is worth it.

In summary, expressing your own feelings, opinions, and needs is not an easy skill. Being assertive means being able to set up clear boundaries and look after your rights. Being assertive is to have a clearly defined goal and strive for its implementation, it is self-respect, taking care of own affairs, but also taking into account the interests of other people, being aware of own possibilities, advantages, but also disadvantages and limitations. Assertiveness means not being easily influenced and pressed by the surroundings. It means having and defending your own values.

Undoubtedly, assertiveness is a crucial element in upholding your inalienable rights and is vital to your well-being.

CHAPTER 5

Develop and Maintain

"It is not hard to make decisions once you know what your values are."
Roy E. Disney

You do not need to have everything to possess something — however, you need your own core values. Once you define your personal values, you discover what is truly important in the way you live and work. Your personal values are a central part of who you are and who you want to be; you can use them as a guide to make the best choices. Values are filters based on which you create your inner picture of reality. Common values play an essential role in society, as they sustain and strengthen social order, motivate action, and also determines people's behaviour. Values should determine your priorities and to help you see if your life is turning out the way you want it to. They exist, whether you recognise them or not. Values are usually stable. Nevertheless, as you move through life, your values may change/adapt to the realities of life. Considerable variation in values can cause conflicts, both within the individual and on a wider scale.

This is why keeping in touch with your values is a vital and ongoing process.

The process of discovering your personal values involves not just discovering what you are passionate about, but also finding out what is really important to you. A good way of starting to do this is to look back on your life and to identify when you felt really good, confident that you were making good choices. Identify the times when you were happiest, when you were most proud. Identify when you were most fulfilled and satisfied. Identify what has been your greatest accomplishments and what has been your greatest moments of efficiency. Also, what has been your biggest failure. What has been your highest moment of inefficiency and why? Likewise, personal values are related to our preferences; however, they are more than preferences. They are part of our existence, this innate part that makes decisions, and which we sometimes call the real self. The more we understand ourselves, the more self-aware we become and the easier it would be to live a successful life.

Another reason why personal values are so important is because it becomes clear to us when we are experiencing a conflict of values. If you have ever felt truly frustrated or angry about something, it is likely you were experiencing a values conflict. This is where there is a conflict with what is actually important to you. Sometimes, just understanding why we feel frustrated can help us move forward.

Another example of a values conflict might be when we are living a life according to someone else's values or fake values.

This is very common among family members. Often children pick up their parents' values instead of their own. When a child takes over the values of his parents, and this is the case in most cases, he also takes over most of their patterns of behaviour, traits, and beliefs. You see, this is where children may have been pushed into a high pay profession when they secretly want to concentrate on something different. For example, the law or medicine could be very important for their parents (due to social status), but not for their children. An adult who acts from the position of a child becomes, with age, fixated on staying with the fake values that separate him from the true self. So, it is crucial that you check on whose values your action is based on; yours or others. It does not mean to renounce what was and is still valid, but to verify and explore its source.

Although your personal core values may not exactly match anyone else's, they still help you determine your surrounding culture. Most people consciously or unconsciously use personal core values to select friendships, relationships, and business partners. Your core values also help you wisely manage your personal resources, such as time and money.

Defining the hierarchy of your life values is something that cannot be forgotten while working on creating happiness and fulfilment. How often do people go in a completely different direction than they would like to go only to realise that this is not the place where they want to be. Recently, I noticed in some certain repetitive pattern. He is a guy; he has a beautiful wife, children, and a good job. He spends a lot of time in this job wanting to earn more and more. When he returns home, he is tired and does not give his children and wife enough time. He works, works, and works. So, a few years passed, until at some point he realises that he lost a piece of his life. He looks around and sees that his children have already moved out of the house. There is no contact with them; they do not even call him. His wife does not want to talk to him anymore as they no longer have common themes. The thought strikes him that he did not want to have such a life. He lost what it was most important to him for work, which now gives him no satisfaction. Sounds familiar?

So, by increasing your knowledge about yourself and your own values will help to nurture your personal growth. As Tony Robbins says, "what you value determines what you focus on." So, it will narrow your focus and will help you to achieve your personal and professional goals. Every goal you set for yourself, when it is consistent with your values, will truly be your goal and will certainly generate a lot of motivation. Very often people follow their goals by working on the success and happiness of other people. Knowledge about your values will make you choose what is important for you, not just for others. It will allow you to follow the right direction. Every decision and action, when it is consistent with your highest values, makes you feel happy. And vice versa, lack of happiness is usually caused by failure to meet all the most important values.

Take your time to identify your values as they will become your personal sources for successful living (personal and professional).

So, how to avoid conflict of values:

1. Notice when someone else is trying to force their opinion or values onto you.

2. Remember, no matter how encouraging they may sound, and how good their intentions could be, other people do not know what is important to you.
3. Start to think about what is important to you and less about what others think.
4. It is okay to have different values and opinion for other people.
5. Only you know what really matters to you.

Examples of values: accountability, ambition, achievement, compassion, consistency, diversity, equality, empathy, freedom, fairness, faith, growth, health, honesty, joy, openness, respect, recognition, love, stability, security, serenity, trust, and wisdom.

I use my personal core values as decision guidelines that keep me true to myself. Knowledge about my highest values provides me with the opportunity to do what gives me profound satisfaction and a lot of real happiness. And the goals I set always flow from the depths of my heart. My personal values deeply affect the way I create and maintain a relationship. I surround myself with good and positive people. I have ended an unhealthy relationship, and I am doing what is in line with my own principles.

So, by working on yourself and on your values, you will achieve great satisfaction. It will help you to be a better version of yourself every day. It will help you to identify your mission and vision. Finally, you will live in harmony with yourself.

Once you know what is important to you, you will never waste your time on things that do not matter.

CHAPTER 6

Idealist

"Perfectionism is self-abuse of the highest order."
Anne Wilson Schaef

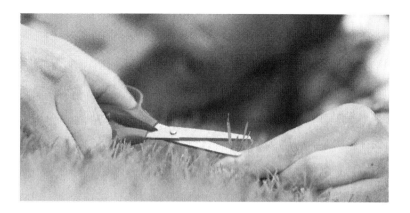

An idealist is a person who is guided more by ideas than by practical considerations. An idealist has faith in people, despite unpleasant experiences — also, faith in own values and goals. An idealist always has reason to live. He has something to hold when everything wants to overcome him. An idealist is a person who is guided by high-level principles and goals and is able to pay the price for their implementation. So, being an idealist and a perfectionist means the same?

Perfectionism can be defined as the pursuit of unrealistic, extremely high demands on oneself, which in the case of failure can lead to a decrease in self-esteem. A perfectionist is someone thorough, conscientious, meticulous, and hardworking. It would seem that it has only advantages.

Answering the question whether being an idealist and a perfectionist means the same, we can say that an idealist and a perfectionist share one thing, namely the desire to cross the border of human possibilities and achieve unreal things.

However, perfectionism...

According to the free Encyclopaedia "perfectionism, in psychology, is a personality trait characterised by a person's striving for flawlessness and setting high-performance standards, accompanied by critical self-evaluations and concerns regarding others' evaluations. It is best conceptualised as a multidimensional characteristic, as psychologists agree that there are many positive and negative aspects. In its maladaptive form, perfectionism drives people to attempt to achieve an unattainable ideal, while their adaptive perfectionism can sometimes motivate them to reach their goals. In the end, they derive pleasure from doing so. When perfectionists do not achieve their goals, they often fall into depression." (https://en.wikipedia.org/wiki/Perfectionism_ (psychology). Perfectionism can make you feel depressed, frustrated, anxious, and even angry, especially if you constantly criticise yourself. So, perfectionism is a dangerous personality trait. It can ruin your self-confidence and it can also result in misery, dissatisfaction with your life, and can even lead to suicidal thoughts.

Having a problem with perfectionism is a lot like having a fear of making mistakes or being imperfect. Perfectionists are terrified of making mistakes; they tend to get bogged down in details and spend a lot of time worrying about the little, micro things. So, they often cope with their anxiety of making mistakes by procrastinating, as it might feel easier to procrastinate rather than spending hours trying to do complete some tasks. However, many perfectionists are obsessed with achieving a certain standard, to the point where they pay little regard to their health and relationships. This also involves the risk of burnout. They often bring their work struggles home and taking out the frustration at their loved ones. Besides, they can look for more suitable partners, but none of them would meet their expectations. Some of them may even impose their high standards on their family. They expect their families to uphold similar standards as them. This high pressure not only weighs down their relationships, but more importantly ruins everyone's happiness.

People develop different personality traits as a result of the experiences they have been through. Perfectionism, for example, could be developed as a result of feelings of inferiority or of being less than others. Another important reason for developing perfectionism is the pressure to hide our deficiencies. We all believe that if we do everything perfectly, no one will trouble to unfold what is hidden behind the mask. No one will acknowledge our limitations. However, a perfectionist knows them all and will judge and criticise himself/herself more than anyone else.

I do remember the time when I tried to be perfect. I tried to fit into the picture-perfect world. I have expected everything and everyone around me to be perfect too. Perfect wife, mother, worker...perfect woman. I tried to get a perfect house, perfect clothes; even I wasn't sure if I like it. By trying to fit in, I lost my own style if I ever had one. I was concentrating on being perfect, but not on being happy. I thought that I would be happy once I become perfect. But I could not reach it. The little, irrelevant things were the greatest reason for my unhappiness. I never felt proud of myself. I felt that I need to set up and achieve a new goal. Likewise, I do remember the anxiety to start something new; the fear of judgment if I would not be able to succeed.

So, my perfectionism deprived me of seeing and feeling the joy of small but very important things in my life. Also, it makes me tired as no one was able to do things for me because it would not be good enough. I was not able to rely on anyone, trust anyone. I was the only person who was able to do everything, even though it was not perfect too.

I thought that being perfect would make me a better person. Better? ...in whose opinion. Now, I know that a sense of inferiority caused my perfectionism. By being perfect, I tried to hide my past as I was ashamed of it.

However, today, I know I am who I am because of the past. I know what is important in my life. I have my values and my own belief system, a new belief system. I do believe that you do not need to be perfect to be good. Your past, spotless house, brand clothes, and high position do not define you as a person. What would define you is the way you treat others. Your willingness to take responsibility for your own life and your commitments in everything you do.

If you would like to be perfect, be perfectly imperfect.

Socially, we tend to praise and reward people who are ambitious and set high goals. Very often it is the perfectionists who achieve these goals. So, when is the time to work on your perfectionism? When it ceases to serve you, and negative emotions dominate over your actions. As long as perfectionism does not hurt you, you would not feel the need for change. So, it is important to acknowledge and to be aware of the negative characteristics of it.

Examples of "dangerous" perfectionism:
1. Lack of satisfaction and sense of fulfilment
2. A sense of insufficiency
3. You are your own biggest critic
4. You need to control everything as no one would be good enough to do it for you
5. You need more time or you do things more than once to make sure it's completed perfectly
6. You think that you should look perfect, work perfectly and live perfectly.

For example, a perfectionist housewife only considers a perfectly vacuumed and washed floor. If there is one crumb on it, she recognises that there is a complete mess in her home. There is no intermediate state. Another example, "I do not know enough, I am not enough. I'm not ready yet. I need to read this book and finish that course. I will be able to start only when I get this certificate..." Unhealthy perfectionist is still preparing for life; he/she is never ready to take action. That is why many of their activities remain only in the area of planning. In their world, it is all or nothing; there is nothing intermediate.

How to work with perfectionism:
1. Make mistakes
2. Be authentic
3. Set priorities, acknowledge your achievement
4. Do not criticise yourself and others
5. Be your own friend, appreciate yourself
6. Ask for help
7. Appreciate the help of others
8. Give them the right to make mistakes

Some form of perfectionism requires specialist support. We can deal with unhealthy perfectionism, although it is not a straight path. The best form of work is psychotherapy. Therapy is based on accepting yourself with your limitations, showing your own excessive requirements, refuting erroneous beliefs about the expectations of other people. It is worth spending time on such work because getting rid of perfectionism allows you to live more calmly and improve your relationships with other people, which will significantly increase the quality of your life.

Don't forget to seek professional assistance if needed. We are asking for help to remain strong, not because we are weak.

CHAPTER 7

Tolerance and Loving you

"Beauty is not who you are on the outside; it
is the wisdom and time you gave away to save
another struggling soul like you."
Shannon L. Alder

Lack of self-confidence and the way we see ourselves is the misery of many people; it hinders at work, at school and, above all, hinders social contacts. The reasons for the lack of self-confidence can be temporary or may have been in our lives for many years, and it is difficult for us to get rid of them.

The image of oneself is a very complicated process based on many different factors, including the culture of the society in which we live. We all experience setbacks in life and that can really blow all the self-confidence out of us. Not only those events that we went through, but more importantly, people who we meet and who influenced the sense of our value. Excessive criticism in childhood from our family, teachers, and peers leaves a permanent scratch in our minds, and it is difficult to get rid of it. Under the pressure of criticism, we start to doubt your own abilities, and sooner or later, we give up on ourselves. We fail ourselves. We fail to realise our own desires and give up on our big dreams. We allow our action to depend on the opinion of others. The willingness to be liked and accepted makes us do everything that others do. We become a puppet in the hands of others; we make bad decisions and act against ourselves. People manipulate us, and instead of appreciating our sacrifice, they use us as much as possible. Many of us run an internal battle between what we think, feel, and what we do. Often, we keep some semblance, pretend to be someone else, we are not ourselves; more so, we are afraid to be ourselves. We are wearing a mask. The strongest reasons for this attitude is lack of self-belief. Believing in yourself is about being certain that you are going to do whatever you want to, even against others. Against their beliefs, opinions, and valuation.

It is interesting that most people around you are not interested in you at all, and certainly not every detail of your appearance and not all what you do and say. People have their own affairs and, in reality, they are interested only in their own lives. Even if they sometimes say something malicious or laugh, they forget about it, and they do not pay attention to it. But, because you are sensitive to the reaction of others, it means a lot to you. Likewise, some people have difficulty accepting someone's success and bravery; courage to oppose and fight for their goals. Because they are scared of changes, they do nothing by themselves. They feel frustrated and unhappy. They pour their anger and disappointment on others, especially those who are consistent and persistent in their actions. Those ones will try to prove to you that you are frail, they will try to deprive you of your self-confidence and your decency.

You can defeat them, but how?

Try to approach every day with greater distance and with greater indifference. Focus on the tasks you have to do and be the best at what you do; learn and develop your skills. Do not think about yourself badly. Forgive your past self. Accept that sometimes good people like you make bad choices. It does not mean you are bad; it means you are human. Love and accept yourself. Take care of your affairs. Find your passion and sacrifice it as much time as possible. Also, choose your company carefully. Surround yourself with positive people, especially those who fully appreciate you as you are, not as they want you to be. Choose those who motivate, inspire, and respect you. And don't give up on yourself. Do not give up on your dreams. Build your personal and professional life based on your strengths. Appreciate your own progress. Do not look for the approval of others. Listen to your intuition and believe in your abilities. Help others believe in themselves and grow. And be thankful for everything and everyone in your life, including impolite, tough people too. They are great reminders of who to not become.

It does not really matter what other people think you should be doing with your life. All that matters is that YOU know what you are doing with your life.

Tenacity

Furthermore, if you have tenacity, you are very determined and do not give up easily. Tenacity means persistent determination. The determination to stand for yourself personally and professionally. Tenacity is the quality displayed by someone who just would not quit, who keeps trying until he reaches his goal. A determined person is persistent and does not pay attention to obstacles. He is sure he will succeed, even if it seems impossible to others.

Despite not the best life experiences and being full of complexes and internal constraints, I had a dream. I always wanted to be accepted for who I am. I always wanted to prove that you do not need to be rich or to have a known name to be valued, treated with respect, and succeed. I always wanted to prove that your past does not determine your future. I always wanted to prove that we all have the power to create our lives. I was scared but determined. I was confident in my decision. I was conscious of my "WHY," and today, I am fulfilling my dream.

Today, as a professional but also as a woman with personal experiences, I am sharing my message with you.

Be aware that you would not be able to wear a mask regularly. Be proud of yourself and what you have gone through. Be professional, but give yourself the right to be real too. Stand on your side and defend your values, as your personality, values, and belief system also determine your professionalism. And remember, you would not be able to do a good job if you act against yourself.

Also, remember that how you perceive yourselves affects how others perceive you. This is not about your external image. It's about who you really are and what you think about yourself: If you feel incompetent, others will see you as incompetent too. If you do not believe in yourself, the lack of faith also will be visible. What we think about ourselves is the strongest message that wanders the world. Do you want to change the attitude of others to yourself? Change your way of thinking about yourself.

Respect yourself and you will be respected. Believe in yourself and others would believe in you.

Self-love

Before you can receive love and respect from others, you need to love and respect yourself. Self-love is important for numerous reasons. It has a profound impact on how we see ourselves and how we treat ourselves. Besides, no one has a better understanding of your thoughts and needs than you do. When you love yourself, you feel good and valuable, deserving of happiness. The more good, beauty, and values you see in yourself, the more values you also consider in other people. However, in order to be able to give away love, first notice it in yourself, take it out of yourself, expand and strengthen it. Give it to yourself first before you direct it towards others. It is difficult to give something that we do not have...

If you want to change the world, change yourself.

CHAPTER 8
Mental Hygiene

Hygiene in the area of mental health is now as important as health in general. Knowledge about how to take care of your own mental health, how not to overload our defence system, becomes the primary factor in the prevention of mental illness. I always wondered why people talk freely about personal hygiene, but a mental one raises anxiety. As we know, it is easier to address physical needs when mental presents not only a serious topic, but also serious difficulties. Many people mistakenly think that only those who suffer from mental difficulties need to think about mental hygiene. They do not think that they also need to look after their own mental state to remain mentally well.

Mental health problems can affect the way that people think, feel, and behave. A mental health problem can feel just as bad, or even worse, as any other physical illness because it is manifested not only by bad mood. Also, under the cover of physical symptoms, there are problems with the soul.

Mental health problems can have a wide range of causes.

The following factors could potentially activate poor mental health: childhood abuse, trauma, neglect, social isolation or loneliness, experiencing discrimination and stigma, bullying, long-term stress, social disadvantage, poverty, domestic violence, or other abuse as an adult.

In addition, there are also many jobs threatened with occupational burnout, in which employees most often experience depression related to their profession.

For example:

Care assistant: A typical day for the carer of the elderly is feeding, bathing, walking, and personal hygiene. Often, older people are not able to express gratitude or appreciation for their hard work because they are too ill. Due to the lack of positive feedback, carers often suffer from depression.

Social workers: Dealing with abused children, dysfunctional families, alcohol problems, etc., is extremely difficult for every social worker. His work usually does not end after 8 hours. Stressful situations and a great responsibility for health, as well as the life of others, are reflected in his own health.

Nurses, doctors, psychotherapists: These people help us to make our physical and mental health in an immaculate condition. Long night shifts, diseases, injuries, the death of the patient, accusation of the families of the injured persons, all this causes that suicide attempts in this professional group are much more frequent than in other groups.

So, what mental hygiene comprise:

1. Dealing with your inner chatter.
   Inside each of our heads lives a chatterbox that runs all day long. It prompts us of everything we have done wrong, makes negative assumptions about what everyone else

thinks of us, and tells us that we are never good enough. It is full of negativity. No one can see it or hear it, but it is powerful. So, what does the chatterbox hold that makes it powerful? It holds limited beliefs, past experiences, feelings, emotions, and opinions. So, the most challenging part of mental hygiene is to be aware of the chatterbox and our own thoughts. Your thoughts are responsible for your feelings. You can feel anxious, sad, unhappy when reacting or concentrating on negative thoughts. Once you take control of them, you are in a better place. How to do it? Once you experience negative feelings, you have to stop for a moment and check what is going on in your mind. It is imperative to be aware of how you feel, act, react, and why. Once you are aware of the negativity, it is important to switch it for positivity. It is good to write your thoughts down, acknowledge and to replace them with an optimistic one. It would be difficult at the beginning, but definitely will help you to concentrate on the positive aspect of your life, which is very important for your mental wellbeing.

2. Belief system
   Belief system is a set of principles that not only helps us to interpret our reality, but also it is something that affects our lives. We all have a different belief system based on the way we were raised, the political system we lived, religion and the belief system of those who we were surrounded by, such as parents, teachers, and friends. So, it is clear that it is something that we learnt, copied, or adopted during our life. So, we can change our belief system if we need

to. It could happen unconsciously when we are under the influence of others or consciously when we examine them for evidence. So, we have to check if our current system is helpful or not and to explore alternatives. It is important to be aware that our belief system drives our behaviour, is responsible for our action and the way we treat ourselves and others. You need to remember that no one needs to accept your belief system except you. Also, you need to remember that we are all entitled to have our own belief system and there is no better one. Your own one is the best one for you. Change of your belief system will take time, but it will help you live life as you want to.

"No one can make you feel inferior without your consent."
Eleanor Roosevelt

3. Positive mental attitude
   We all have good and bad days, and that is ok; it is normal. It is normal to experience different moods and different emotions too. But what is important is to not focus on it. After one or a few difficult days, you may experience a miracle. You may feel very happy, full of energy and motivation. So, positive mental attitude is to acknowledge and accept what we are experiencing and focusing on positives instead of negatives. More importantly is to check what is going on in our life, why we feel the way we feel. Every day is different; we can have a busy and challenging time at work, relation problems, health difficulties, so we can have a reason for the way we feel. But it does not mean that we would not

be able to feel better tomorrow, or once we overcome our difficulties. Stay positive even on bad days. I know you will say it is impossible. However, it is possible. What you need is to find a few things that you are grateful for every day. Do not allow one bad moment to overtake your whole day. Do not allow one bad day to overtake your whole week, and do not allow one bad thought to overtake your whole life.

4. Work-life balance
   "Women, in particular, need to keep an eye on their physical and mental health, because if we're scurrying to and from appointments and errands, we don't have a lot of time to take care of ourselves. We need to do a better job of putting ourselves higher on our own 'to do' list." - First Lady Michelle Obama

According to the encyclopaedia, "Work–life balance is the term used to describe the balance that an individual needs between time allocated for work and other aspects of life. The term 'Work-Life Balance' is recent in origin, as it was first used in the UK and US in the late 1970s and 1980s, respectively. More recently, the term has drawn on some confusion; this is in part due to recent technological changes and advances that have made work and work objectives possible to be completed on a 24-hour cycle. The use of smartphones, email, video-chat, and other technological innovations has made it possible to work without having a typical '9 to 5 work day'."

Work-life balance is a daily effort to make time for family, friends, personal growth, and other personal activities, in addition to the demands of the workplace. Because many of us experience personal, professional, and financial pressure, work-life balance can be challenging. Also, the demanding work culture and the increase in working hours can have a significant effect on an individual's lifestyle and a detrimental impact on their mental state. Especially, women's roles in the workforce with many women/mothers working from home. Part of this change is due to an increased need for dual incomes in many families, but also because many women hold high qualifications and want to grow professionally. Moreover, the current developments in technology allow people to work from any place and at any time. On the one hand, this helps us remain professionally active, but, on the other hand, it is dangerous as there is no limit on working hours. Preservation of the balance between running the home, bringing up children, and working at the same time is very difficult, especially if everything takes place in one place – the home. Also, when you are constantly bringing work home.

A lack of work-life balance can affect us in many ways; physically, emotionally, and financially. The particular balance we need between our work and personal life varies depending on our sex, age, health, as well as personal and professional goals. However, no matter what you do for a living or what responsibilities you may have outside work, it is imperative to preserve the balance if you want to achieve your personal and professional goals. Further, if you want to remain physically and mentally well.

So, how can we achieve a better work-life balance?

The first step is to think about our current challenges and their impact on our personal and professional lives. Next, we need to create a plan that allows us to achieve the right balance. We can do this by:

- Creating realistic boundaries between our work and personal lives, setting clear expectations with our employer and family.
- Prioritising tasks. Focus on the most important and sensitive thing, whether it is at work or at home.
- Having "my time." Having time to relax, meet friends.
- Being assertive, not only by saying "no," but also by communicating our needs.

Having a successful career is an important part of many people. However, it is also essential to find a good balance between our job and personal life. This is not only important for our wellbeing, but it also ensures we are getting the best out of both aspects of our life. By maintaining the balance, we will remain physically and mentally well. More so, we will achieve more in personal and professional life.

In summary, set up clear boundaries between work and private life, prioritise tasks and be assertive. Look after yourself, as you are responsible for your own wellbeing.

"The pressure of an increasingly demanding work culture is the biggest and the greatest challenge to the mental health of the general population."
Unknown

5. Proper rest

You need to be aware that sleep deprivation could have a detrimental impact on your wellbeing. It could cause immune, digestive, and respiratory difficulties. You may feel tired, irritated, and unable to concentrate on any task. It could affect your mental state. You may experience mood swings and difficulties in decision making. Constant tiredness can affect your sex drive. Lack of sleep can lead to mental health illness, especially depression and hallucinations. The recommended sleep length is 7-9 hours. Moreover, the quality of your sleep is also essential. So, do not forget to keep away everything that can destroy your sleep, such as laptop, mobile phone, etc.

6. External appearance

   As you know, clothes do not make the man. But they affect the way we feel about our self. Probably more than once, you heard the saying: "how they see you, they write you." If we look good, not only are we better picked up by others, but most of all we feel better in our own body, which makes us more confident, happy with life and positive attitude. Our self-esteem also rises. So, take care of your external appearance. Find your own style. Dress elegantly but not richly. It is not about the price or the brand just about your image and your personal and professional appearance.

7. Physical fitness

   Along the same lines as personal appearance, physical fitness has a huge effect on mental state. If you are out of shape, you might feel uncertain and unattractive. This will definitely affect your mental state.

   Some people say that the body and mind are separate. As you may know, I will disagree. The state of your mind affects your body. So, if you are tired, anxious and low in mood, you do less. If you do less, you feel lower or even depressed. If you feel depressed, you will miss things that you normally enjoy; for example, cycling, swimming, and you may feel worse. And vice versa. If you are not active, spending long hours at work, your mood could drop down. You may lose interest in spending time outdoors, with friends or family. So, consequently, you will become withdrawn and depressed. So how to be more active every day. Do not worry; it is not about being a gym champion.

It is about using stairs instead of the lift, to leave a bus one stop earlier and to walk more, to play with children or animals. If you like physical exercising, that is great. If not, go for a walk and breathe deeply. Focus on here and now, at this moment. Start with small steps and notice the big difference.

So, by physical exercise, you will improve your physical appearance, and you will increase your energy level. It will increase your confidence, and you will be able to contribute more to the community. The more you contribute to the world, the more satisfied your life would be.

8. Support network

For most human problems, there are no easy solutions or medication. Even if you can get the best professional help, it turns out to be insufficient for many people coping alone with difficulties. Very often, access to a professional is difficult or involves a great deal of concern for the interested person. In such situations, people can and find support in groups of mutual help. Within these groups, they share common issues, concerns, and information that provide them with significant help in healing. They gain understanding from people who have similar experiences.

Support network enhances the quality of our life, and it helps us to deal with difficult life events and to overcome our barriers. It helps us to focus on our goals, strengths, and to keep a positive self-image. It provides a sense of belonging and external security. It helps in building strength, hope, and sense of value.

Taking care of someone and supporting others also brings satisfaction, which is important for our happiness and health.

9. Keep learning
   Learning new skills can give us a sense of achievement. It can increase our confidence and self-esteem, help build a sense of purpose, and help us connect with others. It doesn't have to mean getting more qualifications. There are lots of different ways to bring learning into our life.

We might sign up for a course you have been meaning to do at the local adult education centre. We might learn a new language, dance, yoga, mindfulness, and cooking, especially healthy meals. We can take on a new responsibility at work; we can become an expert in our field and enhancing our knowledge by reading new books. Learning often involves interacting with other people. This can also increase our wellbeing by helping us to build social relationships.

10. Environment

Excessive untidiness causes a lot of stress and can affect every side of your life. Clutter can distract you, weigh you down and, in general, it invites chaos into your life. Tackling the clutter can be seen as an impossible and very stressful task. By devoting a little of your time to getting rid of the clutter in your life and maintaining things relatively clutter-free, you will gain the rewards of comfortable living areas, reduced stress, and more productive life. The best way to tackle the decluttering of your home, your workspace, and your life is to take things one small step at a time. Once you successfully decluttered, you have to be aware of the risk that clutter will certainly begin to sneak back into your life. You must be vigilant in tidying it out on a regular basis, or it will just take over your life again.

"Think this is bad? You should see the inside of my head."

CHAPTER 9

Live Your Experience

"If you're ready to stop living a fear-based life,
you have to decide that your dreams are more
important than your fear of failure. Make the
decision today to overcome fear and start existing
as the most joyful, successful version of yourself
possible."
Tony Robins

Fear is one of the most basic human emotions that help protect us. It makes us alert to the danger and prepares us to deal with it. Feeling frightened is very natural and helpful in some situations. Fear can be healthy if it protects a person to stay safe around something that could be dangerous. But occasionally, fear is irrational and causes more difficulties than needed. People tend to avoid the situations or things they fear. But this does not help them overcome fear — in fact, it can be the reverse. Avoiding what is frightening keeps it strong. People can overcome unnecessary fears by giving themselves the chance to learn about it and increasingly get used to the thing or situation they are afraid of. Fear is an unpleasant emotion caused by the threat of danger, pain, or harm. Fear is a part of the human condition and an unavoidable part of our life journey. Fear is worrying about something that has not happened and thinking about worst-case scenarios if it would. The physical and emotional discomfort of fear is often worse than actually experiencing the fear. Fear is a distorted picture of the future created by our mind. Also, it could be given to us by our parents, siblings, and friends that we should be afraid of, even if we have never experienced danger at first hand. Because they are afraid of something, they make us scared too. Also, if they do not believe in something, they could place their own disbelieves on us. I do remember to be told that no one will help me for free, men do not cry, etc. Most of my generation heart those wisdoms on a regular basis. I am sure you would find something that represents the community where you came from too.

It is true that we are all "coming from" somewhere. The first and the closest surroundings are very important as they could leave a trace in our psyche for longer than we think. And, for me, it was something big in it. Being a small and unsecured kid, being told that I would not be able to achieve a lot become a life true for me. Despite my numerous successes, I always felt that it is still not enough to prove that I can, and I am achieving something. I always felt internal pressure that I need to do more. I need to prove that I am worth it.

However, I do remember the day when I was told that "it's never enough for you, you still want more and more." It was a critical moment in my life. I found it very difficult as I never thought that way. As you already know, I felt that I need to. I asked myself… can I stop? What would happen if I stop?

My big fear was what would happen if I stop. Stop being perfect, stop being and doing things for others. What would happen if I say NO? There were not any other options than to test it. I do remember the huge anxiety, tension in my muscles, sweatiness, accelerated heartbeat, stomach cramps, and an ocean of tears, invisible tears. I do remember the uncertainty and fear of what would happen.

"The invisible tears are hardest to wipe." Unknown

The devil did not turn out to be scary as he was painted. The other side of my tears turned out to be beautiful.

This feeling of inner freedom and the peace that has prevailed in my heart has changed my life. I have found the happiness that has always been so close and, at the same time, so far. I knew it that I can push the horrible pressure away, I knew it that I have the right to say No. I knew it that I do not need to prove my worth. I knew it that I can create my life based on my values, rules, and wishes, but I was scared of making a decision, more of taking action.

... I would like to, and I'm afraid... What to do: Fight for yourself or give up? Who never experience this type of dilemma?

As Tony Robbins said, we are unable to accomplish our biggest goals because of our fear. Fear is the biggest limiting factor preventing us from making decisions about what we really want. Fear causes us to make excuses and distracts us. Also, fear is responsible for our internal struggle. An internal conflict is the feeling of contradictory motives, where the implementation of one excludes the implementation of the other. Being influenced by the internal conflict, we feel torn between two different desires, knowing that we can only fulfil one of them. It is not easy to make a decision and, for some people, even impossible. Without finding a solution, they withdraw themselves from the conflict by distracting and concentrating on other matters, pretending that "there is no case." There is a belief that "everything that I will do will be bad anyway, so it is best not to do anything." Do you know that there have been cases in which the accumulation of this type of conflict, resulted in a lack of motivation to get up in the morning and stand up to the new day? The internal struggle and lack of ability to be YOU can cause you to live in constant stress.

The life under persistent stress could cost you a lot, and it could cost health and even life. Long-term stress is thought to be a factor in high blood pressure, heart disease, obesity, problems with the immune system, some cancers, and diabetes. Stress might worsen many skin conditions, contribute to hair loss, mouth ulcers, and increase the risk of having stroke. Long-term stress is the reason for mental health difficulties, including phobias, anxiety, and depression. One of the major risks of depression is suicide. How many people are losing the battle? Many of them are famous, well known and successful. Many of them we admire, and we know personally. Many of us can see their glory, but we cannot see their stories.

But what if there was a way to turn fear into fuel?

As Brian Tracy said first, you must realise the role negative thinking plays in feeding your fears. Thinking affects feelings and behaviours. If we think badly, we also feel unpleasant emotions, such as sadness, fear, anger, helplessness, and shame. Also, we often rate positive events as unfavourable; we are serving ourselves unpleasant sensations. From negative thinking, generating unpleasant feelings is the simple way that leads to destructive behaviour: resignation, surrender or escape.

What else does negative thinking mean?

If we think negatively about ourselves, other people, the outside world, and it is continuous thinking, accompanying us constantly, then the consequence will be persistent emotional tensions, depressed mood, fatigue, mental overload, and lower self-esteem. Negative thinking is harmful to our mental health, personal and professional life.

How to deal with negative thoughts?

First of all, they should be observed. Negative thoughts are most often automatic. Second: stop the negative thoughts and replace them with positive ones. You have to believe that you are the creator of your thoughts and feelings, and only you can change them. Stopping and replacing negative thinking is not easy. Immediate effects are not to be expected, because a change in thinking is a skill that requires hard work. And most importantly: do not give up after the first unsuccessful attempts to change your mind. Changing negative beliefs is a challenging work, but worth the trouble.

So how can we turn fear into fuel?" When you put your brain to work on a positive task, there is little room for negative thinking. This is turning fear into fuel. Also, getting out of your comfort zone, turning fear into excitement and anticipation is another way to use fear as fuel towards your success," said Brian Tracy.

Why being real is so scary? Why expressing true emotions is so difficult? Why being assertive seems impossible? Why do we not make our dreams come true?

Probably out of fear. Or because we are too busy with doing what we do not enjoy and what we consider to be our duty. Maybe because of the lack of confidence? Perhaps also because someone told us that we are not good enough? Maybe because we cannot imagine a different, better life? Or probably because we never dreamed about it?

You may say that there is no place for dreams in real life. But everything starts from dreaming, isn't it?

We are all wearing a mask, and we all have beauty hidden within. It is time to reveal it. It is time to be YOU.

I have fulfilled so many of my dreams; achieved my goals. Finally, I have reached the point where I have a safe and warm home, a job I like and in which I am constantly developing. I am not scared of showing my real emotions. I am not afraid of saying no and asking for help if needed. I am able to acknowledge my achievements and to admit my mistakes. I am professional, but I am human too.

"People see the glory, but they don't know the story."
Michelle Watson

CHAPTER 10

Allow Yourself To Be Yourself

"To be beautiful means to be yourself. You don't
need to be accepted by others. You need to accept
yourself."
Bindi Irwin

Especially women, much more often than men, surrender
completely to the environment, ignoring their own self completely.
They have a strange tendency to take the pain of the whole world
over their shoulders. This, unfortunately, makes it difficult to be
yourself. They blame themselves for everything from the youngest
years of their lives. Do you remember from your past how guilty
you felt because your parents got divorced, or you were not good
enough at school, not perfect enough? It is constant worrying,
constant torture. Women, like no one else, love to worry about
existence, appearance, whether they satisfy their guy, whether
they are good mothers, daughters, and workers. They get lost
in this trap of satisfying everyone, completely forgetting what
a wonderful feeling it is just to be yourself just for a change.
Fortunately, in the life of many women comes a moment that
they just say enough! I will not apologise for who I am and what
I want. After all, not everyone must love me. If you do not accept
me, or if you do not like me, it is ok.

How to be yourself?

The point is to understand that each of us is unique in their own individual way and does not have to feel guilty about it, or to apologise for it, even if everyone else considers you to be the strangest person in the world. Each of us has the right to like what we like, to have our own opinions, disagree with the opinion of others, and fully accept yourself. Absolutely no one has any right to tell us who we are to be. This is our life, and only we will struggle with what our every day brings, not everyone else. Diversity is beautiful, colourful, and we have the right to be diverse.

Being yourself is also the ability to give up toxic relationships, or other relationships. At work, of course, we have to comply. However, in everyday life, in relationships with friends or close relationships, everyone has the right to be themselves.

You probably heard that friends get to know each other. When everything is fine, it is great, and when something starts to fall, you cannot count on anyone. There is a similar relationship in business. In many situations, there is no query about respect and acceptance of another person. How often do you hear about people who give their best and still met dissatisfaction and rejection? Then they blame themselves that maybe they could do something differently, that perhaps they did not do everything right. Do not apologise for being who you are. Be bold, brave, and beautiful. Be yourself. Make yourself a priority in your life, do not apologise for making choices against convention, and make plans without deferring to anyone and expect more.

Do not waste time and life to play roles imposed by others. Be yourself.

Don't change
so people will like you.
Be yourself and the
right people
will love the real you.

CHAPTER 11

Their Stories

It's not what's happening to you now or what has happened in your past that determines who you become. Instead, it's your decisions about what to focus on, what things mean to you, and what you're going to do about them that will determine your ultimate destiny."
Tony Robbins

I have had the opportunity to meet amazing professionals. All of them are successful people and expert in their fields. They kindly agreed to share of being professional and being human too. Their stories show that your past does not define your future. Moreover, your past and your experiences allow you to understand people better and to see more than others can.

1. Professional, yet human
   On an average day, there are various skills that I have to deploy in working with clients and their families, as well as the various professionals and organisations involved in my field of practice. All at the time, I needed to maintain my professional identity, which was also shaped by the person I am. Like each individual, who I am is influenced by many micro factors, such as my personality, gender, and age,

and their interconnections with macro variables like race, culture, and worldviews.

An integral part of my role, as a specialist mental health worker, is to competently relate with people, whatever their backgrounds, if I am to support them effectively. Doing so requires that I keep myself informed of circumstances that can mitigate or worsen the difficulties of people who have mental illness, through gathering information, analysis, and decision-making.

Work processes require a high level of objectivity, during which professionalism can obscure the humanistic element of personal impact. There is a plethora of guidance cautioning workers to 'separate the personal from the professional.' Unfortunately, this is often translated to mean that there is no room to extend humane characteristics, like compassion, when interacting with patients who are mentally unwell. Yet, it is our personal interests that should not get in the way of our professional responsibilities to vulnerable people, not our humanity! With a naturally reflective personality, this is a regular day to day consideration for me.

Recently, I was involved in a complex discussion with a Paediatric Registrar and a Children and Adolescent Psychiatric Consultant who respectively requested that I undertook an assessment under the Mental Health Act 1983, with a view to detaining a child in the hospital for the purpose of forced treatment. We had an extensive debate, as I spent significant time explaining the child's rights within the legal framework, which does not provide for treatment of physical health, and was the basis of their referrals, 'urgent life-saving treatment, after a serious suicide attempt.' Whilst I understood the situation, and the philanthropist within me also wanting to preserve the life of all children, my professional boundary was defined by law.

On and on, our conversations went, with me offering guidance on alternatives such as legislation about a person's mental capacity and how they may be treated against their will, if deemed in their best interests. Unfortunately, this then led to gridlock between the two doctors as they disputed which one of them needed to act, and when. I left them to continue their debate. However, part of me wanted to follow up (the personal, driven by human feeling) with a phone query to know what they eventually decided regarding the child in the end. The other part of me (the professional, underpinned by specialist training) accepted that I had carried out my function, by considering their referrals, advising them appropriately, and clarifying that there was no further need for me to be involved.

This case occurred a few months ago, but every so often I find myself wondering what happened to that child, and the reality is I may never know. A reality which I accept, though it doesn't stop me thinking about the child, hoping, praying even, that the right decision was made at the right time. As a parent with a child of a similar age, the case was even more emotionally moving for me, because I did not want to accept that there are children who are finding life so unbearable that they would want to die. Yet, I remember that there was a time, many years ago, when as a child I too wanted to die.

Grace Kelly, Specialist Mental Health Professional

2.

When Beata first asked me to share my experiences of hiding real emotions and adapting to the needs of others for her book, I agreed to it straight away. Firstly, because Beata is a great woman, and secondly, because the subject is very close to my heart.

During coaching sessions with my clients or development workshops on assertiveness, working with emotions, self-esteem, and fear, I frequently observe certain behaviours. We, women in particular, tend to push our needs to the very end of the list of what is most important. Since childhood, we have been taught that we have to be polite, obedient, and compliant... The effects of this type of upbringing can be seen in many grown-up women...

Personally, I was made to believe that too. For a large part of my life, I was torn between what I wanted and what was expected from me by others. Today, I can say that I have come a long way to finally understanding that my needs are very important, and that to be true to yourself is the recipe for a satisfying life. It would be difficult to achieve this without taking part in trainings, reading several books on the subject, working with specialists, and most importantly without putting the knowledge I had gained into practice.

I often hid my real emotions, even from myself. When I heard my "needs," I felt a great sense of guilt. Today, I understand many of the mechanisms that used to determine my behaviours. I know what has resulted in the conviction that thinking about myself and my expectations was something wrong... I am convinced that it is worth trying to get to know yourself, to get to know your instincts and their causes. I myself lived in this confinement for more than 30 years before seeing the light.

When you are focused on the outside world, on the sensitivity to what others say, what others need, what others think is good and bad, you stop understanding yourself and your emotions. In order to satisfy your parents, siblings, grandmothers, aunts, neighbours, peers, you stop understanding yourself and your emotional needs. You try to look for acceptance in the eyes of others. Trying to satisfy others, despite it being futile, means you feel internally torn, and you grow in the sense of incomprehension and lack of acceptance.

Personally, I have experienced a strong suppression of my own emotions. "The nail in the coffin" turned out to be the divorce of my parents, for which I had "waited" a few years – while observing how they were growing apart. When it happened, I felt a great sense of guilt. Very often, the children feel guilty when their parents' marriage breaks down. When it is accompanied by a lack of communication or explanation, the division into different camps, the lack of support from our loved ones, the breakdown of certain contacts – this can result in a powerful blow to your emotions. To some extent, a self-locking mechanism protects you from suffering. It might seem ok, but if it takes a long time, it can contribute to an inner sense of sadness and loneliness.

I remember my reaction when I was already in my thirties, and I was told – "Listen to your emotions…" What bloody emotions?–I thought. This was completely incomprehensible to me, as if it was said in a foreign language. Frustrations, a sense of regret and failure – are largely the result of living outside of your own emotions. When you are growing up without a role model, conversations about feelings and needs, acceptance that something can be important to you, even though it is not for someone else – you see the effects of pushing aside your own needs and putting the needs of others on a pedestal.

Nothing, however, has been lost. Such customs, emotions, and experiences can and should be worked on and new ones, which support us, developed. Today, I live much more consciously, I understand many of my emotions, and therefore I live AUTHENTICALLY. Thanks to that, I act assertively because I know my own limits. I live consciously because I make my decisions in accordance with my expectations and needs. I build healthy relationships where I can live in harmony with myself and be open.

Thanks to my own experience and knowledge, I consciously support other women in discovering themselves, their emotions, needs, and assertive attitude. This allows them to live an authentic life. I believe that understanding your own emotions and recognising their worth, living in harmony with yourself, gives you a great sense of fulfilment.

I feel great joy when I see that my openness, even to difficult issues, allows others to dare to be authentic. When my almost seven-year-old son talks about his emotions, gives them a vent, shows joy, tears, anger – he is given space to do so. I try as hard as I can to provide him with that opportunity. Of course, I do realise that this is not always the case, but as a conscious person, I can see it and verify it.

Freedom… This is the most powerful thing a person can offer to herself. And this is what I wish for you.*

Katarzyna Machlowska – Hulok Business and Life Coach

3. My Invisible Mask - Illusive to change
   I was a bass player in a band, which not only gave me an ego boost on stage, but I was incredibly introvert, which also dented my confidence. I had a huge social life, but I also found it hard to connect with people due to suffering from depression and social anxiety, which was a big factor in this part of my life.

   I had many family problems, as I was very much the black sheep of my family. I found myself staying in the same situations, as not only trust was the biggest issue, but there have also been numerous times where I felt like I have had an invisible mask. I will recall them back to you in this section; this has truly shaped the person I am today. The first time I found myself not as my true self was when I was in a band; I was a bass player and really incredibly passionate about it. I was very extrovert on stage, but very introvert off stage affected a lot of the relationships I had with other people.

So, hiding my true emotion was a huge part of my life at that moment as I would hide it through my music; it had trapped me in a way that I had no emotion but within my music.

The second time this happened in my life was when I had lived with my ex-partner who has my little girl - this happened when drugs, drink, and prescription medication for depression got involved. It's because, as I was experiencing a sense of needing and belonging, it had trapped my sense of being conscious of my own feelings and thoughts. I was incredibly emotionless, and I didn't realise how much it had affected my life as I was so fully concentrated on looking after my little girl. I was always giving more to others instead of myself, so my self-esteem had really become damaged and broken. Part way through the relationship, I had found out that I was being cheated on, which not only made me feel worthless, but I felt like my confidence had been chipped away even more. I purely didn't understand how to show my emotions due to being knocked down time after time.

Through these experiences, I have found myself learning not just that trust isn't built in with everyone, guilt and shame is something that is pushed on to us and that we have the power to change anything in our lives.

Chris Greenfield – Mindset Coach

4.

I woke up in the dead of night, I couldn't breathe, and I couldn't move. I was gripped vice-like around my chest, and like a fish out of water, I was gasping for air. Each breath was painful, and I was dying, dying. I heard those words running through my mind. Slowly I tried to breathe, breathe through the pain of my lungs trying to expand and contract. I awoke in the accident and emergency, fighting for my life. The antibiotics didn't work, I had contracted sepsis, my life force was slipping away, and I was growing weaker and weaker.

I remember the sensation of being suspended between life and death hovering weightless, and the thought came to me, I had to choose between life and death. I summoned every ounce of my remaining will and told myself, I will not die today, and I must breathe. I don't know how long I had been lying on the trolley in accident and emergency, while the doctors fought to save my life, but I do know that I chose to live, and that day, my Mindfulness practice saved my life.

How did I end up in that situation? The answer is simple, work stress. The more overloaded I became, the harder I felt I had to work, if I could just do the next thing and the next thing I could manage, and I could help all the people that needed my help. My life had gotten out of balance, I had ignored the signals my body was giving me. I was too busy saving others, giving everything and leaving nothing for myself. Eventually, it caught up with me. My colleagues saw me as a capable professional and someone with a great deal of energy and ability to get the job done, change things and make it better. I worked in an environment that did not support me to be my authentic self, yet it drew from me the essence of who I was to deliver a service in a way that I felt I could deliver with integrity, but at great personal cost to myself, no one saw that.

What I learned from the experience of my body just giving up is that 'you can't pour from an empty vessel,' attending to one's needs first is vitally important for one's own survival. I practice mindful meditation, and a general definition of mindfulness is being in the present moment, paying attention on purpose and noticing being aware of your thoughts and responses to those thoughts moment by moment. Mindfulness starts with the breath, and by focusing attention on the act of breathing slowly in and out, we bring ourselves home to the body, and we can notice what is happening in our minds, our bodies, and our environment.

When one is in a state of awareness, one can decide to choose to do things differently, think differently, and take different actions. We are human beings, yet we spend our time as human doing, often acting at an unconscious level. We often go through life not thinking, just doing the next thing and the next thing, not stopping to be in the here and now, in the present moment.

As I lay on the trolley in the accident and emergency department, I recalled the words of Jon Kabat zinn, 'you only have moments to live.'

I was acutely aware that my life had been condensed down to a single moment, and that each moment lay in the next breath, as I clung to life from breath to breath, not knowing if each breath was going to be my last. Every fibre of my being was concentrated on the breath, and I understood the power of what it truly meant to be fully in the present moment. Each moment became my whole world, and my entire life lived in every single act of choosing to take the next breath.

Viktor Frankl, in his book, Man's Search for Meaning, states, 'you can take away everything from a man, except his ability to choose how he responds.' Viktor Frankl was a man who ended up in a concentration camp and had everything taken away from him. His life became a mere existence, yet he chose how he was going to respond to his situation. Living only in the moment and finding something to be grateful for, to give him hope and to choose life, he survived the terrible ordeals in the concentration camp.

The techniques of breathing I had learned in my Mindfulness practice became my emergency tool kit, and I was able to use it to build a bridge back to life. My sister had been told by the consultant to prepare to say goodbye to me. I survived.

When we practice mindfulness, we can develop clarity, resilience, and focus as we slowly develop an attitude of acceptance. By being fully present at the moment, we learn how to shift from a doing mode to a mode of being. By changing our mind mode, we begin to see with fresh eyes. By attending to our feelings and observing our thoughts, space is created to allow a different perspective. This is an act of self-care and self-cherishing. We must cultivate this habit in our daily lives so that we can become better versions of ourselves in order to serve more fully our families and our communities. Self-care is never selfish; you can't pour from an empty vessel.

May Whyte, Mindfulness Coach

5.

We see the world, not as it is, but as we are - we see, hear, and experience the world based on our own pre-existing values & beliefs and when challenged, of course, we are hard-wired to defend our beliefs because we must be right - right?

This kind of social exchange is happening every day all around us. It is an essential part of communication and of our learning - and of course, we engage in open honest dialogue - right?

We listen and respond - right? But what happens if we don't - or can't bring ourselves to have those dialogues? What happens if we choose to stay silent? If we choose not to engage with what is troubling us? Well, inevitably, conflict and resentment will arise.

Conflict is the direct result of a breakdown in communication, and most of us will do anything we possibly can to avoid conflict, even when it makes us deeply unhappy.

If unchecked, our burning resentment will fan the flames of the outright destruction of our relationships. How many relationships have gone up in smoke over one, or another, or both parties refusing to address the issue at hand? Why do we fear confrontation so much? We will go to extreme lengths to avoid it, and we routinely do more to avoid pain than to walk towards pleasure. I admit I have in the past been guilty of culling more than one person from my address book without allowing them the opportunity to defend themselves - "If thine eye offends thee, pluck it out!"

Isn't it easier to remove the 'offending article' and get on with life free from the all upset? Remove the source of the pain? Well, no, actually it isn't.

Unless you can forgive and release the hurt you feel, you will always carry tiny fragments of it that will cause you pain every time you go through a similar situation, and you will find yourself going through those familiar situations again and again and again and again.

So what is it that we are really afraid of confronting, and what is it that we are really angry about?

In truth, we carry the pain of the past, our wound - in the secret self-limiting stories that we have made up about ourselves in our search for validation: we are unlovable, incapable, powerless, unworthy, take your pick. We unconsciously revisit our past hurt, and in conflict, we project these feelings onto the situations that touch our wound. The more deeply the wound is pressed, the greater the pain and the less we think that we can ever forgive - but to move past the pain, we must learn to release and forgive. We must take responsibility in understanding that it is the projection of our own creation that is causing us conflict and distress.

Similarly, we have the power to release ourselves from this pain. To find a different way. To create another story. Forgiving ourselves first is just the start. It is the only way to heal your past and your future. It's a journey of rediscovery that ultimately brings you peace, and this manifests by touching everyone in your life; past, present, and future.

So for those of you out there, culled from the worn pages of my address book-

"Please forgive me, I'm sorry. Thank you, I love you."

Caroline Partridge – Clarity & Communication Coach

6.

My name is Feyi Jegede, a Fitness Expert and Trainer, Inspirational Speaker and Published Author and Single parent to 4 amazing children. Thank you to the beautiful Beata Bikowska for allowing me to be open and to contribute to her book.

Honesty has always been the best policy, or so we hear people say... but how many of us really believe this? How many of us want to take a mirror up close and look at our reflection? The invisible mask that we hide behind, which is our emotions.

For many people who know me and my personal journey to date, you will see that everything that I do has stemmed from me being open about my Life – the breakdown of my marriage, becoming a single parent, losing my home and everything else that I have gone through (such as Overcoming limiting beliefs, Fear, and Doubt).

Being open about your emotions is not something any of us finds easy to do, but it is the best way to be healed from pain and hurt and to live freely in life.

Before I met my husband, I would say that I was the type of person that was a ball of emotions, dealing with rejection, anger, and pain. Growing up in a home where we did not really express ourselves openly meant that I grew up with a lot of bottled emotions that often manifested itself in anger. As I got older and became more aware of this, I began to work on myself and the causes of my anger, and I realised that I wanted to live a life where I could be more open and honest with the people around me.

So, by the time I got to my teens, I had developed the habit of wanting to be open to everyone I met and tried very hard to work on many of my issues. Now, by the time I met my husband in 2006, I got married and had 3 beautiful children within 3 years, and I felt that we had developed a loving and trusting relationship between the two of us.

But sadly, our marriage broke down after 3 years, when my husband walked out on me. Looking back now, I realise that the cause of the marriage breakdown started when my husband stopped being open to his emotions and became quiet about his feelings – his feelings of feeling overwhelmed, inadequate, and frustrated in the marriage. Whereas at the beginning of the relationship, we had both been very open, honest, and communicative. By the end of our marriage, he had now shut down from communicating about his feelings and often skirted around discussing our issues.

I know that, for men, being open about their emotions can be a very difficult thing – especially men that feel bound by their culture and upbringing. But for me, being open about my emotions and what I was feeling – if not to the outside world – but at least to myself is what I believe has helped me to heal from the hurt and the pain of the marriage breakdown. My trust was shattered, my belief in people was questioned, and my perspective on being an honest and open person was called into doubt. For me, the hardest thing of all is when you try to hide the mask of your pain behind the mask of calm. But I worked my way through that because, deep down, I realised that by being open and not hiding my emotions, or even hiding the fact of my failed marriage from people, allowed me to re-build my heart and soul.

"The hardest thing of all is when pain is hidden behind the mask of calm" – Sergei Lukyanenko.

I totally agree with this quote because I know that it takes great skill and great courage to do this.

So, Today, from this experience, I have developed a more loving and open relationship with my children, where they all understand the importance of being open, honest, and real with each other (while respecting and valuing each other's opinions). Of course, this is something that is never ever easy to do, but the benefits of doing so are far immense. We often spend many quiet times together as a family talking about how we feel and, most importantly, learning how to let go of our past, our pains, and our wrongs.

Today, I believe that it is essential to work on your emotions, understand yourself and be true to who you are – no matter how this may appear or seem to others. In a world that is constantly trying to make you something else, I know that this can seem very hard to do. Even today, I still have to deal with different emotions that may arise from my ex-husband, my disagreeing siblings, from difficult work relationships, from challenging situations that arise, from arguments at home and so many things that can sway and move your emotions. But I always remind myself never to let my emotions overpower my intelligence; and no matter the situation, I always try to stay Positive and Strong.

And how do I manage to do what I do – to juggle my life, my children, to home-school them and run a business? A question that I often get asked, and my answer to this is "I Acknowledge my weaknesses, I Focus on my Strengths, and I am honest and open with myself." And you can only do that when you are ready to be open, honest, and frank with yourself and emotions... and to finally take a long, hard look at the person staring back at you in the mirror!

Conclusion

You will probably agree with me that we have different roles in our lives. We are wearing different masks, depending on the role. We are wearing caps, helmets, and we are covering our bodies in uniforms to become the best example of the role. We become partners, parents, employers, employees, business owners, law officers, and lifesavers. We are holding huge responsibilities, depending on the role as well as the weight of what is hidden behind our mask. Unresolved conflicts, crises, unfulfilled dreams, but more importantly our emotions. Emotions that have a huge impact on our functioning in everyday life, whether personal or professional.

The current image of strong and successful individuals created by the media leaves no space for talk about the price that many people pay for being picture-perfect. It leaves no space to talk about real life. The real life, which is far from the colourful picture in the tabloid. The real life full of challenges, fears to face, and lessons to be learned. Thanks to them, you are who you are. Do not be ashamed of them, be grateful to them. They did not happen to you, they appeared for you, for your personal and professional growth. So, grow up and help others to grow too.

> "It is literally true that you can succeed best and quickest by helping others to succeed." – N. Hill

Acknowledgement

I would like to say "thank you" to everyone who I met in my life. It is true that we meet people for reasons. Some will stay with us, and some will disappear, but all of them will leave their mark in our life.

In relation to the development and production of this book, I am very grateful to:

- My husband Artur for his love, patience, and support
- Author, Publisher, and Mentor Michelle Watson for inspiring, believing, and their ongoing support
- Nicki Vee for providing the foreword and helping me to develop my passion further
- Grace Kelly, Katarzyna Machlowska-Hulok, Chris Greenfield, May Whyte, Caroline Partridge, and Fayi Jegede for contributing by sharing their stories

Also, I would like to acknowledge my deceased friend Christine Noyes, the woman who inspired and touched many hearts. I miss you.

Biography

Beata Bikowska is a Social Worker, Health and Life Coach, Multi Award Winning Motivational Speaker and Author, Wife, Mother, and Grandmother. Born in Poland, living and working in England from 2006.

Registered in Health and Care Professionals Council and Polish Psychologists' Association. Beata Bikowska has been working with people for over 25 years and is extremely passionate about assisting individuals to set and achieve both their personal and professional goals within all areas of their life from learning, employment, relationships, and their own personal wellbeing. She has gained extensive experience across the Health and Social Care sector working within a wide range of roles from a Staff Nurse, Social Worker, and most recently Health and Life Coach. She has had the honour of accompanying people in various moments of their lives, from sadness to joy, from resignation, falling, fighting, and finally victory, to whom many of us, including herself, can relate to.

So, as a Success Coach and Mental Wellbeing Expert, Beata helps individuals in all sectors to define their life, occupational, and pro-health goals, as well as help them to define their resources, action plan and, above all, help them achieve and live their desired life. The ability to assist individuals to consciously manage their mental state and discover their hidden potential, manage it and achieve personal or professional success, is what propelled Beata to create her programmes and strategies, which now enables her clients to excel beyond their imagination. Beata not only has the knowledge and professional experience, but also life experience that many can relate to as she suffered greatly due to lack of belief in herself that had a significant influence on how she once lived and felt. Beata was able to overcome this lack of confidence and limiting beliefs to achieving her goals and becoming a successful entrepreneur, and these are the many tips and strategies that she now shares with the world.

Beata believes strongly that one should never stop believing in others and encourages that you should believe in yourself and live the life you want.

37195010R00058

Printed in Poland
by Amazon Fulfillment
Poland Sp. z o.o., Wrocław